D0099689

Properties of Matter

Shape, Size, and Volume

Arthur Best

Cavendish
Square

New York

Published in 2019 by Cavendish Square Publishing, LLC
243 5th Avenue, Suite 136, New York, NY 10016

Copyright © 2019 by Cavendish Square Publishing, LLC

First Edition

Website: cavendishsq.com

This publication represents the opinions and views of the author based on his or her personal experience, knowledge, and research. The information in this book serves as a general guide only. The author and publisher have used their best efforts in preparing this book and disclaim liability rising directly or indirectly from the use and application of this book.

All websites were available and accurate when this book was sent to press.

Library of Congress Cataloging-in-Publication Data

Names: Best, B. J., 1976- author.
Title: Shape, size, and volume / Arthur Best.
Description: First edition. | New York : Cavendish Square, 2019. | Series: Properties of matter | Audience: K to grade 3.
Identifiers: LCCN 2018023586 (print) | LCCN 2018025013 (ebook) | ISBN 9781502642493 (ebook) |
ISBN 9781502642486 (library bound) | ISBN 9781502642462 (pbk.) | ISBN 9781502642479 (6 pack) |
Subjects: LCSH: Shapes--Juvenile literature. | Size perception--Juvenile literature. |
Concepts--Juvenile literature. | Volume (Cubic content)--Juvenile literature. | CYAC: Shape. | Size. | Concepts.
Classification: LCC TL782.5 (ebook) | LCC TL782.5 .B4275 2019 (print) | DDC 516/.15--dc23
LC record available at https://lccn.loc.gov/2018023586

Editorial Director: David McNamara
Copy Editor: Nathan Heidelberger
Associate Art Director: Alan Sliwinski
Designer: Megan Metté
Production Coordinator: Karol Szymczuk
Photo Research: J8 Media

Printed in the United States of America

Contents

Each thing has a shape.

A ball is round.

5

Here is a can.

It has ends.

They are circles.

7

A box has edges.

They are **straight**.

9

A size is how big something is.

Here are some balls.

Some are smaller.

Some are bigger!

Some things are **huge**.

Tall buildings are huge.

13

Some things are **tiny**.

These grains of salt are tiny.

15

Volume is how much space a thing takes up.

You can **measure** it.

This ant is small.

Smaller things have less volume.

They don't take up much space.

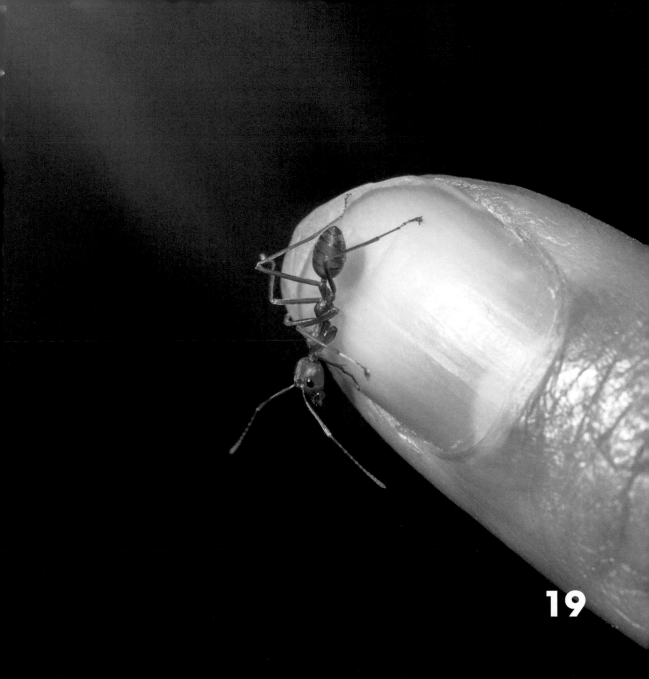
19

This hippo is big.

Bigger things have
more volume.

They take up more space!

21

New Words

huge (HYUGE) Very big.

measure (MEHZH-er) Find the size of.

straight (STRAIT) Not curved or bent.

tiny (TIE-nee) Very small.

volume (VOL-yume) How much space a thing takes up.

Index

About the Author

Arthur Best lives in Wisconsin with his wife and son. He has written many other books for children. His favorite shape is the dodecahedron.

About BOOKWORMS

Bookworms help independent readers gain reading confidence through high-frequency words, simple sentences, and strong picture/text support. Each book explores a concept that helps children relate what they read to the world they live in.